Richard William Church

Advent sermons

1885

Richard William Church

Advent sermons
1885

ISBN/EAN: 9783744745505

Printed in Europe, USA, Canada, Australia, Japan

Cover: Foto ©Lupo / pixelio.de

More available books at **www.hansebooks.com**

ADVENT SERMONS

1885

BY

R. W. CHURCH

DEAN OF ST. PAUL'S
HONORARY FELLOW OF ORIEL COLLEGE, OXFORD

London
MACMILLAN AND CO.
1886

TO

THE REV. ALBERT BARFF

MASTER OF THE CHORISTERS OF ST. PAUL'S

WHO BY HIS FAITHFULNESS AND WISDOM

HAS MADE THE CHORISTERS' WORK

A RELIGIOUS SERVICE,

IN GRATITUDE FOR ALL THAT HE HAS DONE

FOR ST. PAUL'S.

NOTICE.

THE following Sermons were preached at the afternoon Sunday Service at St. Paul's during Advent 1885, in consequence of the absence of Dr. Liddon, who was unable from ill health to be in residence.

CONTENTS.

		PAGE
I.—FAITH AMID CHANGES		1
II.—THE KINGDOM OF GOD—I	.	29
III.—THE KINGDOM OF GOD—II	.	58
IV.—HOPE	.	88

I.

FAITH AMID CHANGES.

"For here we have no continuing city, but we seek one to come."—HEBREWS xiii. 14.

THESE words sum up what was certainly the Apostolic mind as to the position of Christians in this world. They were members, they could not help being members, as we are, of a vast and powerful and complex association—human society; but with all its great attributes it wanted one—it wanted permanence. "The world passeth away" —*is* passing away, as we work or speak. "*Here* we have no continuing city"—we have indeed a city, we have a wonderful and beneficent citizenship, we could not live without it; we owe debts beyond repayment, duties of the loftiest and most sacred kind, to human *society;* but society is with us and about us *to-day*, and to-morrow it and we are to be so much farther on in our road to successive changes, by which *it* becomes something quite different from what it is now, something perhaps which we cannot imagine now; and *we* disappear from life and the visible world. But though "*here* we have no continuing city, we *do* seek one to come." Born amid change—surrounded by change in every form, knowing nothing by experience but change, the subject and the sport of change—the human heart yet distinctly clings to its longing for the unchanging and the eternal. Christians, so thought the Apostle, not only long for it but look for it. "We seek that which is to come;" seek it, believing that we have found it and shall one day reach it.

We do not need Scripture to teach us that we have "here no continuing city"—"that the fashion of this world passeth away"—that nothing "continueth in one stay;" though only Scripture can teach us to seek with hope for that "which is to come." "From the morning till the evening the time is changed, and all things"—the glory of the dawn, the beauty of the sunset, "are soon done before the Lord." In this world of ours, from the first rise of thought, from the first throb of consciousness, no one but has known and owned this inherent necessity of our condition; and human inventiveness and speech have been strained to recognise and record its pressure on the human mind—to evade, perhaps, and disguise the public confession of its inevitable certainty; to express with adequate force the keenness with which it is realised in the individual life. Human pride, knowing it, has tried to defy it; the monuments of these mighty attempts, in Egypt, in Assyria, in India, in China, have survived the centuries: there was once an empire which seemed as solid as the world; there was a city which called itself the Eternal City; and their ruins, like the drifted fragments of a wreck, battered but undestroyed, are the witnesses in our museums, or in desolate places of the earth, to those enormous powers of change over which mortal men once thought to triumph. It is in vain; even the "unchanging East" must go through its revolutions; even the Roman Empire must pass away.[1] The law of unceasing endless change spreads over

---

[1] "So fails, so languishes, grows dim and dies,
All that this world is proud of. From their spheres
The stars of human glory are cast down:
Perish the roses and the flowers of kings,
Princes, and emperors, and the crowns and palms
Of all the mighty. . . .
 The vast Frame
Of Social nature changes ever more
Her organs and her members, with decay

all present and visible things, the greatest and the least. Change, subtle, imperceptible, universal, is the puzzle and the riddle with which philosophy has to grapple;—have things any being, or is it all a becoming, ending as soon as it has begun, a perpetual flux, like a river never two moments the same? are things but appearances, and shifting forms, and not realities? what, under all these accidents of an ever-moving scene, is the substance and foundation which stands firm and upholds them? Great philosophical systems have risen on the answers to these questions; and on their failure to solve the enigma they have been overthrown and fallen, and added fresh illustrations to the uniformity of change. The fact and the power of change—what is all history but the

> Restless, and restless generation, powers
> And functions dying and produced at need;—
> And by this law the mighty whole subsists."
> *Excursion: The Churchyard among the Mountains.*

picture of its vicissitudes and its epochs? What is political wisdom but the recognition of its conquests and the direction of its course? What a monument and evidence is all language of its continuous action and strange results! How do the commonest and most trivial words which we are obliged to use—" Yesterday, to-day, to-morrow "— " hours and weeks and months and years "— witness, like the mottoes on sundials, to its steady current, which none can check or escape? So thought and interest and the atmosphere of opinion, go through the same continuous process of change. Slowly but surely the greatest intellectual revolutions come about. The truths of one age are the questions and doubts of the next, the exploded errors and fallacies of a third. Ideas, modes of argument, assumptions, philosophical methods which governed minds in one century become unintelligible in another.

Even the tests of genius alter. Tastes arise and depart—assert their supremacy and then are laughed to scorn. The masterpieces of to-day fall flat and fail to move us to-morrow. These boasted powers of creative and judicial mind—they too are subject to the empire of change. Poetry and all art confess and recall its power, for they are beholden to it for their noblest and most magnificent materials. Their triumphs have been to arrest and embody its momentary and evanescent flow. They have sought in it the sources of what is most pathetic, most tender, most inspiring—ideals which it has just shown and then taken away, the light which came once and never again. Indeed, they can bind us by a spell, and cheat us into forgetting that irresistible march of change of which they are the evidence. They were before us, and will outlive us—picture and building and poem; and we, fluctuating between the obstinate certainty of the present moment and the knowledge that all is passing, vanishing, tending "visibly not to be;" we, longing for permanence, read into their past and into their future the life which, as it passes, is now our own: like that old man in the poet's story [1] who all his life long had had before him in the refectory at his meals a great picture of the Last Supper, till the picture grew into the reality—

> "And he was fain invest
> The lifeless thing with life from his own soul."

> "Here daily do we sit,
> And thinking of my brethren, dead, dispersed,
> Or changed, or changing, I not seldom gaze
> Upon this solemn company unmoved
> By shock of circumstance or lapse of years,
> Until I cannot but believe that they—
> They are in truth the substance, *we* the shadows."

---

[1] Wordsworth's *Lines on a Portrait*, note. The story is there, and in Lord Mahon's history, told of Sir D. Wilkie in the Escurial. In the later editions of Rogers's *Italy* Mr. Rogers tells it of himself, in a monastery at Padua. Mr.

Such things touch us, as they well may. But what are these to the instances, when we meet them, of the changes of our moral nature—to a life which grows poorer with its years—to the strange declensions of character, the chilling of enthusiasm, the quenching of love, the falls of the strong, the uncharitableness of the good, the failure of a great promise, the shaming of a great past? what are passing years, failing strength, and coming death to the sight of altering and dying goodness?

"Here we have no continuing city." We are all of us under the unalterable necessity in one way or another of change. It is the absolute condition of existing, now and here. How shall we feel about this fact, as certain as death? how shall we meet it, when we no longer merely know it, but imagine and

Wordsworth observes (*Prose Works*, iii. 171) that this wants explanation. Lord Houghton has told the story in some fine stanzas—*A Spanish Anecdote*, ii. 281.

realise it?—no longer merely hear of it by the hearing of the ear, but see it with the inner eye of the living mind. It may impress and affect us in many ways. It may darken or it may brighten life; it may depress and discourage, or it may inspire with boundless hope. We may find in it the highest summons to courage or the excuse for the most enervating sentimentalism. We may bow our heads in sullen despair under the yoke of its necessity; we may cease to strive, and throw up the game in the vain attempt to master or to stem it; or we may see in it more gain than loss, and welcome it charged with infinite possibilities of recovery and advance. We may meet it, thankful that we are born under its dominion and its hopes; or we may meet it with the indifference with which we resign ourselves to what is inevitable; or with the regrets which see in it that which has robbed us of what we most loved and trusted, only a companionship with bereavement, decay, degeneracy; or with irritation at its monotony, its fruitlessness, its aimlessness, its undirected and purposeless course. We may meet it in placid submission to the order of natural law, curbing the restless instincts of the soul for something more and better, without ambition for a more stable and unchequered lot, without aspiration and without repining. We may meet it as fatalists, or as idlers, or as those who said, "Our time is a very shadow that passeth away; let no flower of the spring pass by us; for this is our portion, and our lot is this." There is no escaping from the consciousness of change. From the first, men have met it as wise men or as fools—with mockery and with selfish riotousness, or with the serious thought due to one of the master-facts of human life.

"Here we have no continuing city." How

does the Bible teach us to think and to feel about this truth, which often comes upon us so unexpectedly, with such piercing force? The Bible, we know, was written that we, "through patience and comfort of the Scriptures, might have hope" in the changes and chances of this mortal life, as well as in its sins, its temptations, its terrible evils. The Bible, which has told us of the presence and victory of our Lord, of the life and immortality which He has brought to light, teaches us abundantly what to think of change, both in its good and its evil, and of that unchanging glory in which it is to be swallowed up. But is there in the Bible any special guiding for judgment, for temper, for self-discipline, for everyday feeling and everyday behaviour, under the disquieting consciousness of change—any ever-ready counter-charm when the stern facts of change present themselves oppressively, insupportably? Doubtless a sentence from the mouth of Christ, an inspiration of an Apostle, can carry strength and comfort to the soul. But we have that, too, which was a source of teaching and a stay to Apostles, and from the words of which, the words of men though taught by the Holy Ghost, even the Son of Man deigned to draw language for His feeling and thought. We have the Book of Psalms, the mirror of the deepest and most varied spiritual experience, the inspirer of the strongest feelings of religious assurance. In the Book of Psalms we may read how the believer in God may learn to feel and to act when he sees the great currents of change sweep by him, and feels himself borne upon their tide.

I need not remind you how, throughout the Psalms, we meet the impressive recognition of this aspect of life and the world. They are full of the presence, the greatness, the eventfulness of change—change going on for good or for evil, for joy or for sorrow, in outward circumstances, in the inward life; changes physical, material, political, moral; vicissitudes in the fortunes of men and nations, varying states,. perhaps most rapid alternations and successions of feeling in the soul within, in its outlook towards God and things outside it. The writers of the Psalms knew well what change was; they lived under the pressure of great catastrophes, of great failures of hope, of great degeneracies and great disappointments, exposed in their little corner of the earth to the enormous movements round them, ever tempting or troubling them, ever threatening to overwhelm and consume them. And they knew, too, the deeper and more far-reaching changes that come over character and conscience, and man's relations to God, and the varying and never stable scene of man's obedience. They felt as keenly as any despairing or indulgent Epicurean thinker how fleeting are our moments of life, how wide and restless the processes of change. But in this rush and whirl of the things of sense and time the Psalmist had one fixed point. That fixed point was the sovereignty of God—the true, the just, the holy. That amid the changes and chances of visible things, that in the perpetual running out of time, that amid the alternations of life and death, remained ever the same. Of that the Psalmists felt as sure as they felt sure of the vicissitudes of which they were the subject. Blinded, dizzied, perplexed, overwhelmed, like men struggling with a storm, not knowing their road or how the Hand was guiding them, far less knowing how to connect their experience with the secrets and the counsels of His righteousness —their trust was absolute and boundless in that Eternal Rule. Alive as they were to change and all its tremendous powers in things below, yet from their thought of change was never absent the thought of the unchanging Master of all changes. In the heights and in the depths, this was the unfailing stay and refuge of their souls—"The Lord is King."

The idea of the sovereignty of God is the counterpart throughout the Psalms, set over against all that is unsatisfying, disastrous, transitory, untrustworthy, not only in man's condition but in the best he can do in it. The Psalms are always the expression of the will to fulfil God's purpose, though very often of that will baffled; but they always fall back, when that will is baffled, not on despair, but on the conviction that man's "times are in God's hand." That great idea of the sovereignty of God, as philosophical as it is certainly Christian, has perhaps in our days been thrown, by the tendency of opinion and argument, disproportionately into the background. There have been times when it has been made too prominent, at the expense of His other attributes, His justice, His goodness, His loving mercy. It has been urged to justify daring and terrible speculations; and loyalty to it has been thought to require the unshrinking acceptance of the most extreme consequences. But in the writers of the Psalms it is no text for speculation or debate; it is a matter of the deepest practical conviction, of the clearest religious insight. It alone would bear the strain of human anxiety. Without it, for them, there would be no religion; certainly no life, no comfort or refuge in religion. With them it means that God is in the midst of us, taking part in all that concerns and interests men; they ask not how—they know that they could not comprehend it; but from the throne of the universe, guiding, ruling, judging men, as He rules the worlds and all that He has made. That great song of the 100th Psalm, which still, as it has so often done, collects the voices of thousands, is the final expression of this faith—" Be ye sure that the Lord He is God: it is He that hath made us, and not we ourselves: we are His people, and the sheep of His pasture. . . . The Lord is gracious; His mercy is everlasting; and His truth endureth from generation to generation." That other Psalm, which from time out of mind in the Church has been the daily invitation to prayer and praise, is the daily witness and acknowledgment of God's kingdom—" O come, let us sing unto the Lord; let us heartily rejoice in the strength of our salvation. . . . In His hand are all the corners of the earth; and the strength of the hills is His also. . . . O come, let us worship and fall down, and kneel before the Lord our Maker." Here is summed up the answer of the Book of Psalms to time and change and death.

The Psalmists realised that they had "no continuing city" in a way which is far beyond any experience of ours. They knew a state of society which could rely on nothing settled; which was liable at any moment, as is the case still in parts of the world, to be tormented and torn to pieces by insolent and lawless wickedness, to be shaken to its foundations by some frenzy or fashion of false religion, to be crushed down into utter ruin by some alien conqueror. They believed that they were the people of God and had His promises; and yet what they saw was, these promises unfulfilled, recalled, reversed; apparently passing away into nothingness. They, the "people of God's holiness," saw in the midst of them, trampling on all right and holiness, "the bloodthirsty and deceitful man." They, the elect of the Lord of Hosts, saw the "enemy and the avenger" master amid the ruins of God's holy place, and for generation after generation felt themselves the slaves and spoil of the heathen. What wonder that the voice of defeat and humiliation sounds with such tragic repetition in the Book of Psalms. "Hath God indeed forgotten to be gracious? and will He shut up His loving-kindness in displeasure?" But what is the other side of this? It is that, with perhaps one and that only an apparent exception,[1] the voice of unalloyed and uncomforted despair is never heard there. With the wail torn from the heart by shame and agony comes next moment the remembrance of that Eternal King of mercy and righteousness, Whose kingdom endures from end to end, while empires rise and fall, and Whose ear hears with equal certainty the cry of the poor and the blasphemy of the

[1] Psalm lxxxviii.

cruel. In spite of the daily evidence of experience, the wicked flourishing like a green bay-tree, the power of the oppressor, the tongue of the slanderer and the busy mocker; in spite of the long delay, the agonised appeal " How long ? "—" Why standest Thou so far off, O Lord, and hidest Thy face in the needful time of trouble ?"— in spite of all, the foundation stands sure and unshaken by any accidents of mortal condition : " Thou art set in the throne that judgest right. The Lord shall endure for ever; He hath also prepared His seat for judgment. The Lord also will be a defence for the oppressed ; even a refuge in due time of trouble. And they that know Thy name will put their trust in Thee ; for Thou, Lord, has never failed them that seek Thee."

And so with the transitoriness of the lives and generations of men ; nowhere is a keener sense shown of it than in the Psalms. " Man walketh in a vain shadow, and disquieteth himself in vain: he heapeth up riches, and cannot tell who shall gather them." "Man being in honour hath no understanding, but is compared to the beasts that perish." "Thou turnest man to destruction; again Thou sayest, Come again, ye children of men; for a thousand years in Thy sight are but as yesterday, seeing that is past as a watch in the night." "As soon as Thou scatterest them they are even as a sleep, and fade away suddenly like the grass. . . . For when Thou art angry all our days are gone; we bring our years to an end, as it were a tale that is told." What is there to comfort and compensate for this dreary prospect? Nothing but the unlimited trust in God's power and goodness and even watchful care. "My days are gone like a shadow, and I am withered like grass"—*there* is the consciousness which must come to all men sooner or later—a consciousness in the Psalmist's case that these great changes in his lot were not undeserved by a sinner—" and that because of Thine indignation and wrath, for Thou hast taken me up and cast me down." The great revelation of forgiveness and life and immortality was yet to come; but the Psalmist's faith in the Eternal King of the World never wavered. "The days of man are but as grass, for he flourisheth as a flower of the field. For as soon as the wind goeth over it, it is gone; and the place thereof shall know it no more. But the merciful goodness of the Lord endureth for ever and ever upon them that fear Him, and His righteousness upon children's children." "When the breath of man goeth forth he shall turn again to his earth; and then all his thoughts perish." The waste, the throwing away of human souls, of human thoughts, of human affections, is there anything more strangely perplexing in the ruin of death? But the answer is at hand. "Blessed is he that hath the God of Jacob for his help, and whose hope is in the Lord his God; Who made heaven and earth, the sea, and all that therein is; Who keepeth his promise for ever." Men died and were buried, and their children after them. They knew that they must die and be as though they had never been. They walked like shadows in the midst of shadows round them. They felt to the full the swift shortness of life; how soon it was over, how awful its inevitable changes. Yet they did not faint. They knew that over them was the ever continuous rule of Him Who made heaven and earth and all things in them. They doubted not that He keepeth His promise for ever. And so with change and mortality in them and round them, written even on the solid earth and the distant heavens, they broke into the exulting song, "Thou, Lord, in the beginning hast laid the foundation of the earth: and the heavens are the work of Thine hands. They shall perish, but Thou shalt endure; they all shall wax old as a garment, and as a vesture shalt Thou change them, and they shall be changed: but Thou art the same, and Thy years shall not fail. The children of Thy servants shall continue, and their seed shall stand fast in Thy sight."

"Here we have no continuing city" any more than they had. But we know, with a distinctness which all of them had not, of a "city which hath foundations, whose builder and maker is God"—a "house not made with hands, eternal in the heavens." But where is that passionate, delighted, triumphant faith of those men of old? What have we of their joy and gladness at the very thought of God, even amid the tumults of the nations and the overthrows of life, and the certainty that at the best they too must soon "follow the generation of their fathers?" Where is that assurance which they had that "to the godly there ariseth light in the darkness? He shall never be moved; he will not be afraid of any evil tidings, for his heart standeth fast and believeth in the Lord." Where is that "fearful joy" with which they responded even to the terrors of the world? "The floods are risen, O Lord, the floods have lift up their voice; the floods lift up their waves." "The Lord sitteth above the water-flood, and the Lord remaineth a King for ever. . . . The Lord shall give His people the blessing of peace." As surely as they were as we are, in the experience of life, so surely had they this lofty, burning faith, this never-failing, abundant hope. "What reward shall I give unto the Lord for all the benefits which He hath done unto me? I will receive the cup of salvation, and call on the name of the Lord." And so they cast themselves into the arms of God, and were blessed—Oh that we could catch something of the contagion of that faith and hope, as day by day we repeat again and again their wonderful words. This life of ours, locked and dovetailed into the vast framework of social existence, seems so solid that it needs an effort of imagination to think of it shaken. But that effort of imagination Scripture bids us make. It bids us think of ourselves in totally new conditions, in utterly altered relations to all around us; *how* strange, *how* awful, we know not, nor ever shall know here. It bids us think of this world itself, passing through endless phases, till the day of its doom. Search as we will, we can find nothing to rest upon, nothing that will endure the real trial, but the faith of the Psalmists in the eternal kingdom of God—

the faith of the Psalmists lit up by the "grace and truth that came by Jesus Christ." May God grant us the heart to have this faith—the faith of *men*—of men who are not afraid to face their circumstances, who know the greatness of their venture, who are not afraid to trust God, because their hearts go up to Him in longing and self-surrender. "Truly God is loving unto Israel, even unto such as are of a clean heart. Whom have I in heaven but Thee? My flesh and my heart faileth; but God is the strength of my heart and my portion for ever."

II.

THE KINGDOM OF GOD—I.

"Now, after John was cast into prison, Jesus came into Galilee, preaching the Gospel of the Kingdom of God."—ST. MARK i. 14.

"THE kingdom of God," "the kingdom of heaven," are among the most familiar of religious expressions. In the Bible they have applications more or less limited and special, according to the context; just as our phrase "the Crown" carries with it distinct associations, and stands for powers and functions, differing in sphere and attributes, though through them all runs a connecting thread—according as the Crown is spoken of in its legal, or administrative, or political, or personal relations. The kingdom of God brings with it sometimes God's rule over the universe, sometimes His rule in souls and consciences and wills; sometimes we see it revealed in the Church on earth, sometimes we look forward to it in the triumph of its Lord at the end of all things. But "the kingdom of God" is one of the great themes of the Bible; indeed it may be said to comprehend them all. For in its fullest and most complete meaning is embraced all that God is to the things which He has made; all that God is to men, who alone of creatures here are capable of knowing Him and loving Him—all that He has done for them, and is doing for them now. When we grasp all that is implied in our words, "the kingdom of God" is as great a subject to our thoughts as it is natural and common in the language of religion.

The belief in God, the Lord and Ruler of

the world and men, meets us, of course, in the first words of the Bible as much as in the last, and this involves the idea of "the kingdom of God." But the idea of the kingdom of God as one vast system, though always implicitly present to the minds of those who knew and served Him, has not been always equally full and equally clear. Like other great truths of religion it has unfolded its significance gradually. Often obscured, even to good men, by the pressure of things visible and sensible, by trouble, by the struggle and business of life, by the customs and prejudices of men, it only step by step disengaged itself from all that clouded it, and gathered more and more its light and its power over the souls of men. The history of the Bible is the record, among other things, of the growth in definiteness—in full consciousness, in its supremacy over all counter-influences of sight and nature and habit—of the idea of the kingdom of the invisible God. We see in that long and varied history of religion how this great idea presented itself with more and more precision to the minds and imaginations of the servants of God, how it wrought upon their souls, how it gained for itself the distinct and recognised name by which it was henceforth to be known. We may trace, from the early days to the later, how this idea, "the kingdom of God," received, under the inspired discipline of successive generations, increasing illumination, increasing substance and reality, till at length it came to mean all that Jesus Christ meant for us when He came preaching "the kingdom of God," the Gospel of the kingdom.

The outlines of this great object of religious faith and thought, "the kingdom of God," were distinct and prominent in patriarchal religion. When Abraham believed the call and promise of God, when he "lifted up his hand to the Lord, the possessor of heaven and earth," when he made his servant swear by the "Lord, the God of heaven and the God of earth," he confessed, though he had not named it, "the kingdom of God." It was the foundation of his absolute and ungrudging faith—that faith, that recognition of God's claim upon him, by which he is said to have been in a special sense "justified;" that faith by which he became the type and exemplar of generous and heroic obedience—obedience to One Who was worthy of his boundless loyalty, Who was more to him than all the world, more to him than his only son. And this faith of Abraham in the Most High God, "the possessor," as He is called in the story of Melchizedek, "the possessor of heaven and earth," was the heritage left by Abraham to his children and his race. What it was to Abraham in his outward acts we know; what it was to him in the inner thoughts and feelings of his soul is hidden to us. Only we know that he is called by inspired lips " the friend of God." Only we know that One Who knows everything from end to end said of him, " Abraham rejoiced to see My day, and he saw it and was glad."

" The kingdom of God "—the phrase had not yet been uttered; the depths and compass of the thought had not been fathomed and explored; but the whole history of the patriarchs first, and of Israel afterwards, revealed the presence and activity of the belief. In his dealings and relations with the people of His purpose and choice, God, though He was the God of Abraham, Isaac, and Jacob, the God of Israel, was yet remembered as, beyond all that, the King and Ruler of all things: the King and Lord of all men, the " Judge of all the earth." " The kingdom of God" was indeed in a very definite sense the Church of the old dispensation, the Church which was in the tents of Jacob, the Church "which was in the wilderness," the Church whose holy places were at Shiloh and on Zion. There God was recognised, "My King of old." So it was that the memory of the kingdom of God was preserved among men; so it was that the hope was kept alive of that Church universal which was to be, and which was to be at last the visible witness of God's kingdom before the eyes of men. The Jews, we know, misunderstood the meaning of their calling. As is so natural to our narrow and limited thought, to our selfishness and readiness to believe in exclusiveness and favouritism, they were even tempted to confine the kingdom of God to what was but a portion of it. But they might have known better; they might, if they had not chosen to be blind, have read a very different meaning in their great privileges and the wonders which had been done for them. Their own belief, their own professions, witnessed, if they would have heeded, that their Lord was the Lord of all things, of all the families of the earth, of all souls which He had made. St Paul's question might have been asked and answered at any moment of the history of Israel—"Is He the God of the Jews only? Is He not also of the Gentiles? Yes, of the Gentiles also."

Israel believed that the "Lord is King;" they believed, that is, in a "kingdom of God." But words and beliefs may be familiar to us without our always recognising what they mean, and all that is contained in them. A phrase, a doctrine, a discovery, a theory, a deep-reaching principle, the watchword and key-note of a whole philosophy, may be in our mouths, may be in our minds, in a neutralised and inactive state, without life, without influence. The dry seed lies on the ground as dead, and "abideth alone;" it may lie there and perish. But nursed by kindly suns and showers it may wake up and slowly rise and spread into the mighty tree, the glory and delight of the landscape, ringed with its hundred years of growth. So it is with our ideas and convictions. They may go on, the greatest of them, dead, inert, powerless, fruitless, till they have found their interpreter; till they have found that answering sympathy and intelligence of the soul which sees all that is in them with the inner eye of the mind, which illuminates, unfolds, applies them, and animates with them the realities of things. Till this time comes, the highest, the richest of ideas may fall unmeaning on an uncongenial age or an alien temper of society; we may listen to its expression with barren respect, utterly failing to measure its reach or discern its wealth. And so continually, even after it has been living, it may pass under new conditions into the empty formula; and the faith which once had felt and imagined and loved, sink into the languid habit of acquiescence. The history of religion in all times is full of such instances. Thousands have rehearsed the Creed, its stupendous confession of the mystery of the Incarnation and the Holy Ghost, its articles of the Holy Catholic Church and the communion of saints, with but the faintest sense of all that such words carried with them.

And thus Israel acknowledged that the Lord was their King, that He was Lord of heaven and earth; acknowledged it, rebelling, sinning, repenting, relapsing, in His chastisements, in His forgiveness and redemption; acknowledged it with barren homage, with the feeling that God's election was the charter of their security and pride. But the time of enlargement came. One of those great instruments, chosen and raised up by God to be His interpreter and prophet, to say the things not said before, to open the eyes of men to sights not seen before—David the shepherd, David the king, David the Psalmist—rose, under God's teaching, to understand and to tell forth what is really meant by "the kingdom of God." And the thoughts of David, multiplied, diversified, verified, expanded, by the experience and inspiration of a series of devout and holy singers in the Book of Psalms, have taught all generations how to think and to feel about the nature and character of that everlasting kingdom.

Two things appear at once on the surface in this great interpretation of the idea of "the kingdom of God."

1. One is its moral purpose. The kingdom of God is indeed exhibited in the Psalms in all its magnificence, in all its

breadth, over nature and man, over the stars of the sky and the cattle on a thousand hills, and the young ravens that cry unto Him; over the storms of the desert and the waterfloods; over the march of history and the destinies of nations and the secrets of the heart of man; over all that vast inconceivable universe beyond the most distant star. Almost the first utterance of the Psalter is the tremendous warning against the rebellion of the mightiest powers on earth against the "Lord and His Anointed"—"He that dwelleth in heaven shall laugh them to scorn; the Lord shall have them in derision." And the Book closes with those exulting songs of joy and triumph at the splendours of God's kingdom, in the heights above and in the depths below, which seem more and more filled, every time we repeat them, with the strength and the "new wine"[1] of the

---

[1] Zechariah ix. 17.

Spirit of God. "I will magnify Thee, O God, my King; and I will praise Thy name for ever and ever. All Thy works praise Thee, O Lord; and Thy saints give thanks unto Thee. They show the glory of Thy kingdom, and talk of Thy power; that Thy power, Thy glory, and the mightiness of Thy kingdom might be known unto men." "O praise the Lord of heaven; praise Him in the height. Praise Him, all ye angels of His: praise Him, all His host. Praise Him, sun and moon: praise Him, all ye stars and light. . . . Praise the Lord upon earth, ye dragons and all deeps: fire and hail; snow and vapour; wind and storm fulfilling His word: mountains and all hills; fruitful trees and all cedars: beasts and all cattle; worms and feathered fowls. Young men and maidens; old men and children: praise the name of the Lord; for His Name only is excellent, and His praise above heaven and earth." "Let everything that hath breath praise the Lord." Certainly the imagination of these inspired singers grasped, in all its fulness and glory, the outward and visible grandeur of the kingdom of God in heaven and earth. "O Lord our Governor, how excellent is Thy Name in all the world. Thou that hast set Thy glory above the heavens. . . . For I will consider Thy heavens, even the works of Thy fingers, the moon and the stars which Thou hast ordained." And not less wonderful did He seem to them in His doings towards the children of men, in the tokens of His power and judgment in the world, in the strange retrospect over the mysterious history of Israel. "Thy way is in the sea, and Thy paths in the great waters, and Thy footsteps are not known; Thou leddest Thy people like sheep by the hand of Moses and Aaron." "Thou art of more honour and might than the hills of the robbers; at Thy rebuke, O God of Jacob, both the chariot and horses are fallen." We know how such thoughts as these, about His kingdom in creation, in nature, in history, fill the souls of the Psalmists. But the impressiveness of the awe and wonder with which they dwelt on what was outward and tangible makes all the more striking the clearness, the strength with which they discerned, amid all the might and majesty of God's everlasting dominion, amid all its beauty and all its terrors, the supreme and governing power of a moral purpose, of the law of righteousness and holiness and truth. That is the great and determining feature of the Psalmists' varied portraiture of the kingdom of God. It is not merely the kingdom of God the Maker, and God the Ruler of all things; it is even more the kingdom of God in the closest and deepest relations with that moral world which He has called into being in the wills and consciences and affections of men. It is God the righteous Judge, God the Lover and Shield of goodness, God the Consoler, God the Guide, God the Teacher, God the fountain of joy and gladness, God the strength and song of the true of heart, God the Forgiver, God the Healer, God the Helper and the Redeemer, God the compassionate, God the tender and the merciful—"yea, like as a father pitieth his children, even so is the Lord merciful to them that fear Him"; this is He whom the Psalmists recognise and celebrate in the kingdom of God. Theirs is a conviction about that kingdom which, from the first Psalm to the last, knows no blessedness but the blessedness of righteousness, of innocence, of pardon. It is a kingdom far above man's power to influence, far above man's capacity to comprehend or measure; which is revealed to man only that he may understand that its law, "which never can be broken," more firm than the "round world which cannot be moved," than the heavens so far above us, is the law which no change can touch, no might can alter—the eternal law of right and wrong. "The earth is the Lord's and all that therein is; the compass of the world and all that dwell therein. . . . Who shall ascend into the hill of the Lord? or who shall rise up in His holy place? Even he that hath clean hands and a pure heart, and that hath not lift up his mind unto vanity, nor sworn to deceive his neighbour." It is a kingdom in which, amid all its serenities of peace and glory, there is room and care for suffering, sinning, sorrowing man. Its King, "strong and patient," watches with strictest scrutiny, without respect of persons, all that men do and all that men suffer. "His eyes consider the poor; and His eyelids try the children of men." He is a "Father of the fatherless, and defendeth the cause of the widows; even God in His holy habitation." He listens in terrible silence to the wrongs that are done on earth; and the Psalmists feel with certainty that He listens not in vain; that sooner or later His judgments will be manifest. He listens with pity and tender mercy to the humiliation of the sinner; the mysterious power of forgiveness and restoration is in His hands: "there is mercy with Thee, therefore shalt Thou be feared." Such is the way in which the Psalmists develop the idea of "the kingdom of God."[1] They unite in one breath its awful wonder and surpassing glory, and with these its dominant, never absent moral aspects; its correspondence with man's conscience, his troubles and

---

[1] Lord of the world, Almighty King,
Thy shadow resteth over all,—
Or where the Saints Thy terrors sing,
Or where the waves obey Thy call.
     Froude's *Remains*.

wants and fears and hopes. Thus, time after time, the two are joined together. "Thy kingdom is an everlasting kingdom, and Thy dominion endureth throughout all ages. The Lord upholdeth all such as fall, and lifteth up all those that are down." Again, "Who made heaven and earth, the sea, and all things therein; Who keepeth His promise for ever; Who helpeth them to right that suffer wrong; Who feedeth the hungry. The Lord looseth men out of prison; the Lord giveth sight to the blind. . . . The Lord careth for the strangers; He defendeth the fatherless and widow." And once more, His merciful kindness is put side by side with the worlds which He has made. "He healeth those that are broken in heart, and giveth medicine to heal their sickness. He telleth the number of the stars, and calleth them all by their names." This is the characteristic of that Messianic dispensation which is to realise God's kingdom among men. "He shall keep the simple folk by their right, defend the children of the poor, and punish the wrong-doer. . . . He shall be favourable to the simple and needy, and shall preserve the souls of the poor. He shall deliver their souls from falsehood and wrong; and dear shall their blood be in His sight."

2. The Psalmists insist on the moral purpose of "the kingdom of God." What is equally noticeable is the breadth with which they assume and announce its universal character. For they were not insensible to the privileged position of the chosen people. They had all an Israelite's feelings that God dwelt and ruled in Israel as He did nowhere else; their hearts swelled at the remembrance of the greatness of their fortunes, at the pathetic vicissitudes of their most wonderful of histories. "The hill of Sion is a fair place, and the joy of the whole earth; on

the north side lieth the city of the great King; God is well known in her palaces as a sure refuge." "In Jewry is God known; His name is great in Israel; at Salem is His tabernacle, and His dwelling in Sion." "He showeth His word unto Jacob, His statutes and ordinances unto Israel. He hath not dealt so with any nation, neither have the heathen knowledge of His laws." But though they were conscious of their own wonderful election, the heathen were not in their thoughts excluded from the kingdom and care of God. He, their "living Dread, Who dwelt in Silo" or in Jerusalem, was yet the God of all the families of the earth, and for the blessing of all the families of the earth was the blessing given to Abraham and his seed. All that vast sea of nations that surged around the narrow bounds of Israel, so utterly unlike it in language, in worship, in history, separated from it apparently as widely as if they were the inhabitants of another world, was yet swayed and ruled by the All-Holy Whom they worshipped. "It was He that nurtureth or chastiseth the heathen," as He nurtured or chastised them; "it was He that teacheth man knowledge," whether among the chosen of Judah or the strangers who had not learned to call on His name. They, the first-fruits, the first-born of mankind, were but the leaders in the song of praise. "O sing praises, sing praises unto our God; sing praises, sing praises unto our King. For God is the King of all the earth; sing ye praises with understanding. God reigneth over the heathen, God sitteth upon His holy seat. The princes of the people are joined unto the people of the God of Abraham; for God which is very high exalted doth defend the earth, as it were with a shield." We, in our age of the world, can hardly take in the real difficulty of this thought in those old days of local religions and national gods. It was as strange to the Egyptian or the Greek as to the Jew. Nowhere was it realised, except in the Psalmists' high-raised thought; nothing looked like it to human experience or human judgment. But they never doubted. Surely it is as wonderful as it is certain, that in this obscure corner of the world this little people, who but for after-events would be almost lost to history, dared to look forward through the darkness and announce with unwavering faith, in the songs of their worship, the recognition by the Gentiles of "the kingdom of God." "Desire of Me, and I shall give the heathen for Thine inheritance, and the utmost parts of the earth for Thy possession." "Sing unto God, O ye kingdoms of the earth; O sing praises unto the Lord, Who sitteth in the heavens from the beginning; Lo, He doth send out

His voice; yea, and that a mighty voice." "All nations whom Thou hast made shall come and worship Thee, O Lord; and shall glorify Thy name." "The heathen shall fear Thy name, O Lord, and the kings of the earth Thy majesty." "God be merciful to us, and bless us; and show the light of His countenance, and be merciful unto us. That Thy way may be known upon earth, Thy saving health among all nations. Oh let the nations rejoice and be glad: for Thou shalt judge the folk righteously and govern the nations upon earth." And so in the great Messianic prophecy of Him in Whom was to be gathered up "the kingdom of God"—" His dominion shall be also from the one sea to the other, and from the flood unto the world's end. . . . All kings shall fall down before Him; all nations shall do Him service. . . . His name shall endure for ever: His name shall remain under the sun among the posteriors which shall be blessed through Him, and all the heathen shall praise Him."

Such was the image of "the kingdom of God" as it presented itself to the imagination and the faith of those holy men of old. Such is the image which they impressed upon all religion; the image which rose before the mind of the Prophets; never effaced, never forgotten, amid the blinding storms of ruin, in the degradation and bitterness of captivity. "Thou hast been a strength to the poor, a strength to the needy in his distress, a refuge from the storm, a shadow from the heat, when the blast of the terrible ones is as a storm against the wall" (Isa. xxv.) "When the poor and needy seek water, and there is none, and their tongue faileth for thirst, I the Lord will hear them, I the God of Israel will not forsake them" (Isa. xli.) "That they may know from the rising of the sun, and from the west, that there is none beside Me: I am the Lord, and there is none else" (Isa. xlv.) And such was that great preliminary truth which Jesus Christ came preaching when He began His ministry; the foundation of His appeal to the souls of men, the introduction to the deeper and special announcements of what He was to do and to tell us. My brethren, we too are living in "the kingdom of God:" as individuals, as a Church, as a nation, that kingdom, in its awful righteousness, in its vastness beyond our thought and ken, is over us as in the days when the songs of the Psalmists first revealed its wonders to the heart of man. Dimly, indeed, amid the darkness and troubles of the world, we trace its outlines; dimly can we follow the counsels which direct its course. But at least we can try to rise to the height of its greatness; we can catch something of its spirit from the inspired lips of those who have gone before us; we can try to be somewhat worthy of it. We can remember that it is not of to-day or yesterday; it has its roots in what was before the ages, and it reaches beyond their end. Here we are shaken; here we are perplexed; here we are alarmed, perhaps for what we hold most dear and most sacred. Here we see not our path, we miss our way, and the future rises up before us dark and ominous. Have such times never been before? Have not men asked before, "Hath God forgotten to be gracious? and will He shut up His loving-kindness in displeasure?" Ah! the answer to that question was not always what men liked and hoped; but "the kingdom of God" had *not* been turned out of its course, and God had *not* forgotten to be gracious. Oh, my brethren, Christians who have known the triumph of the cross of Jesus Christ, the triumph of His great defeat, let us not fail and shrink as those who do not believe God's kingdom. If troubles seem to threaten, if troubles come, do not let us bear the mind that cowards bear—be downcast and unreasonable, and fretful and violent and unscrupulous. There is no more marked lesson in the Bible than the temper it enjoins for days of disquiet—it may be of pain and fear. Those were not easy days when an Apostle warned his disciples against losing their self-possession, their evenness of mind, and in the stress and hurry of alarm forgetting that their one safety and their one business was to think of pleasing God. "Therefore, we receiving a kingdom which cannot be moved, let us have grace, to serve God acceptedly (to well pleasing) with reverence and godly fear: for our God is a consuming fire." Those were not quiet days—the storm was swelling fierce and loud—when the Psalmist faced the storm—"God is our hope and strength, a very present help in trouble: therefore will we not fear, though the earth be moved, and though the hills be carried into the midst of the sea; though the waters thereof rage and swell, and though the mountains shake at the tempest of the same. The rivers of the flood thereof shall make glad the city of God, the holy place of the tabernacle of the most Highest. God is in the midst of her; therefore shall she not be removed: God shall help her and that right early."

III.

THE KINGDOM OF GOD—II.

"Now when John was cast into prison, Jesus came into Galilee, preaching the Gospel of the kingdom of God."—ST. MARK i. 14.

"THE kingdom of God" was one of the chief subjects of that inspired interpretation of the facts of human life in the Old Testament which we call prophecy. It was the faith, the joy, the hope of the Psalmists, and of those great teachers and witnesses of righteousness who came after them. And in the idea of it which possessed the minds of the Psalmists and Prophets we have two leading features. They thought of it, above all its wonder and greatness, as directed to a moral end and governed by a moral purpose; and, though they connected its presence specially with the history and fortunes of their own chosen race, they conceived of it as a universal kingdom; they extended it, without hesitation or doubt, in its judgments and its hopes, to all the families of mankind. Though the heathen knew not God, though at this or that moment they might be the enemies and oppressors of His people, they, too, were not without their interest in the blessing of Abraham, for they were the creatures of Him Who had said "All souls are Mine." "The Lord is King; the earth may be glad thereof; yea, the multitude of the isles may be glad thereof. Clouds and darkness are round about Him: righteousness and judgment are the habitation of His seat." "Tell it out among the heathen that the Lord is King, and that it is He Who hath made the round world so fast that it cannot be moved: and how that He shall judge the people righteously." I need not remind you that, open where you will, Psalm or Prophet, you will find such words as these. When St. Paul wrote "There is no difference between the Jew and the Greek; for the same Lord over all is rich unto all that call upon Him," he said what sounded very strange to Jewish narrowness; but he said no more than he had learned from the Old Testament, than he found loudly proclaimed by David and Isaiah.

It was plain to St. Paul, but to the society in which St. Paul had been brought up it was unmeaning. Such words lay undeveloped in men's minds, listened to, familiar, but unrealised, unnoticed in their eventful significance, till the process of time cleared them up and disclosed the import with which they were charged. That, of course, which at last fulfilled and revealed their meaning, which brought these words again with fresh force and point into men's memories and hopes, was the coming of Him for Whom Psalmist and Prophet had been so long preparing. Then indeed, as could not but be, the idea, the belief, of the kingdom of God received a light it never had before, and presented new aspects which belonged to that great unveiling of the thoughts of God. For He was among us Who was King in that kingdom. From Him the world was to know, in parable or direct speech, what were the mysteries, the secrets, the laws of the kingdom of God, of which for ages men had heard so much. From Him men were to know all that was to be made known, under the conditions of time and sight, of that invisible and everlasting rule which reaches from end to end, and orders and governs all things. With Him it was a favourite and characteristic expression ; He has enshrined it in the Prayer of prayers; it stood, in His use of it, for all that He brought with Him, of mercy, of blessing, of light; of grace here and of perfectness afterwards. For all were streams flowing from one fountain; all were administrations, powers, creations, presences, influences, of one supreme sovereignty—the kingdom of the God of righteousness, holiness, and love.

Taking the idea as a whole, with special reference to the aspects of it presented in the Old Testament and the New, we may ask what is added by the later to the earlier conceptions of it? And in the New Testament it seems that, while the old features, its supreme moral end, its universality, are retained and emphasised, it becomes at once more definite and tangible, and at the same time more removed to a sphere beyond human experience than it was to the thoughts of the Jewish prophets. For to us it is embodied in the person of the King Himself; that most awful of Beings has been with men; He bears a human name. And on the other hand, all that this world knows of the proofs of greatness and power has nothing to do with Him. What was shown to the eye of flesh, of Him Who "sits on the throne judging right," was the "form of a servant" and the helplessness of the Crucified. He was indeed victorious, with such a victory as human life had never yet seen; victorious over sin, over death, over the hearts of men; but it was not shown on the scene where earthly success shows its triumph and glory. To the last that the world saw of Him, He was the "despised and rejected of men." Strange contrast to the forecast of Messianic prophecy—"Thou art fairer than the children of men; full of grace are Thy lips;" yet another prophecy had warned us what this would look like in all outward appearance.

"He hath no form nor comeliness; and when we shall see Him, there is no beauty that we should desire Him." And, as with the King, so with the kingdom. The world was to see it, and to feel it, as the kingdom of God had never been felt before; yet who could say for certain, "Here is its presence; here is its supremacy"? Evangelist and Apostle never doubt that "the kingdom of God" is indeed "come with power;" they know that it enshrines and makes certain all that man ever hoped for; they feel that they are *in* it and *of* it, fulfilling its tasks, spreading abroad the news of its wonders, wakening up hearts and consciences to discern its tokens. But, as we well know, they go off from the Old Testament idea of a "kingdom"—a power acknowledged upon earth, compelling recognition by visible greatness. All thought of outward greatness has passed into the background in the pages of the New Testament.

They speak, indeed, of the greatness and glories of the kingdom of God; but it is a greatness and glory of an infinitely different order from anything that can ever be seen here. That eternal kingdom, with its risen and glorified Lord, shrinks not from association with what *here* is held to be weak and poor and of no account. Its very emblem is the Cross—earthly defeat, earthly suffering. Its diadem is the crown of thorns. It is here among the souls and the doings of men, " conquering and to conquer;" but its judgments and its conquests, and the awful steps of its march through time, are masked and veiled behind the shows and shadows of this world; sometimes indicated, sometimes partly disclosed, but more than half kept back—too real not to be felt, too much hidden and crowded out by the things of the present to arrest the careless or the worldly heart. It is, indeed, such a kingdom as St. Paul describes in his Epistle to the Ephesians. Day by day in the eternal world, by "the principalities and powers in heavenly places," it is seen how, "in the dispensation of the fulness of times, God hath gathered together all things in Christ, both which are in heaven and which are in earth." Day by day *there* they continually cry, "Holy, holy, holy, Lord God of Sabaoth, heaven and earth are full of the majesty of Thy glory;" they sing the song of Moses and of the Lamb, saying, "Great and marvellous are Thy works, Lord God Almighty; just and true are Thy ways, Thou King of saints. Who shall not fear Thee, O Lord, and glorify Thy Name? for Thou only art holy: for all nations shall come and worship before Thee; for Thy judgments are made manifest." "Alleluia: for the Lord God omnipotent reigneth." So they see, so they rejoice, in the "heavenly places;" but we cannot hear their song, their strain of perpetual praise: here on earth the work and life of a minister and instrument of the kingdom of God is thus set before us: "By honour and dishonour, by evil report and good report: as deceivers, and yet true; as unknown, yet well known; as dying, and, behold, we live; as chastened, yet not killed; as sorrowful, yet alway rejoicing; as poor, yet making many rich; as having nothing, and yet possessing all things."

"My kingdom is not of this world," said the King Himself. It was not only a kingdom of righteousness, a universal kingdom: it would not, as so many expected, as so many desired and took for granted—it would not accept the conditions on which things are recognised and welcomed and honoured as great on the scene of this visible world. It would not as yet reveal all that it was, all that it could claim, all that one day would be known about it. It appealed to men, and challenged their homage, not by signs of power which the world could judge of, not by glory which could dazzle the world, but by those inner forces and tokens which the world imperfectly discerns—the powers of truth and holiness and love and goodness. The whole idea of the kingdom of God in the New Testament is of a kingdom out of sight—the most real, the most certain, the nearest of all things—whose power and presence were to be felt in the world in ways that experience had never dreamed of, but which baffled all experience when it tried to penetrate that impalpable barrier which made the kingdom of God unlike all human things. "The kingdom of God is within you," was the answer when the disciples looked for something which they could point to. "Blessed are the poor in spirit: blessed are they that are persecuted for righteousness' sake: for theirs is the kingdom of heaven." *Theirs* who are of the least account *here ;* *theirs* to whom *here* is assigned the bitter lot of undeserved and unjust suffering. "The kingdom of God is not meat and drink ; but righteousness, and peace, and joy in the Holy Ghost ;" not dependent on outward necessaries of life and strength, but showing itself, "not in word but in power," by those heavenly virtues which mark His rule Who is "King of Righteousness" and "King of Peace ;" "by pureness, by knowledge, by long-suffering, by kindness, by the Holy Ghost, by love unfeigned." "My kingdom is not of this world ;" not of this world's customs, and this world's objects, and this world's instruments ; not of this world's success or this world's vicissitudes ; not amenable to this world's tests ; not resting on what makes this world's strength ; not altered by its revolutions, not failing with its failures: but behind all that this world sees and knows—lasting while men and nations come and go, strangely from time to time breaking in on the course of human affairs—the kingdom of God accompanies this world's history; the kingdom which was sung by Psalmists and imagined by Prophets and announced by Apostles, moving on in its eternal order, whether opposed or neglected or honoured upon earth, until "the mystery of God is finished," and His judgments are made manifest, and "the earnest expectation of the creature" shall be satisfied by "the manifestation of the sons of God."

That kingdom is "not of this world;" but it is *in* this world, and it has its witnesses and representatives in this world, in its varied and manifold aspects and working. It has its witnesses in individual souls. It has its witness, its representative, in the universal Church of Christ. Nothing can be an adequate representative of that invisible kingdom of God; it extends, even on earth beyond even the bounds of the universal Church. But His Church is the designated and appointed recognition of His kingdom, in a sense in which nothing was or could be before He came. "I appoint unto you a kingdom, as My Father hath appointed unto Me; that ye may eat and drink at My table in My kingdom, and sit on thrones, judging the twelve tribes of Israel"—this was His language to the founders of His Church. And from the time that His Church was founded there was that personal relation to Him, the mystery and the closeness of which human words and images have been taxed to the utmost to shadow forth. "Head over all things to the Church, which is His Body, the fulness of Him Who filleth all in all"— I need not tell you how those awful words are developed and illustrated, in the most unexpected ways, in the Epistles of St. Paul and the Gospel of St. John. The Church in Jewish times was part of the kingdom of God by laws and organisation; the Church of Christ by personal union with Him Who is the King Eternal. *That* must indeed be a very real part of "the kingdom of God," which is joined in such a communion with its King. That can be no mere voluntary association of men, thinking and feeling alike. That can be no creation of the will or power of earthly teachers or earthly rulers. Who could call into being so mysterious a fellowship but He Himself whose unutterable love had brought Him into union with His creatures? Who could dare to use such words, unless they came from Him Who sits on the throne of the kingdom of God?

This is that religious society which He has called into being, to be the shadow and the instrument of His kingdom, and which we call the Church of Christ; a religious society existing as a fact among the facts of the world, springing from faith and love to Him, depending on His words, worshipping His name, joined to His Person and nourished by His sacraments, kept alive by His Spirit, continuing on from age to age of decay and change by virtue of an order which has never failed, of a hope which nothing can destroy. This, we believe, is the Church of the Bible and of history; this is the Church of our Prayer-books; this, and nothing less than this; this, and not another. It has looked very different to the outward eye in the many different stages of its actual course here. It has looked like an obscure and unpopular sect; it has looked like a wonderful human institution, vying with the greatest in age and power; it has looked like a great usurpation; it has looked like an overgrown and worn-out system, out of date and ready to fall to pieces; it has been obscured by the outward accidents of splendour or disaster; it has been enriched, it has been plundered; at one time throned above emperors, at another under the heel of the vilest; and it has been dishonoured by the crimes of its governors, by truckling to the world, by the idolatry of power, by greed and selfishness, by their unbelief in their own mission, by the deep stain of profligacy, by the deep stain of blood. Yes, "the treasure" was in "earthen vessels" in a very different sense from what the Apostle meant; it was in the hands of mortal and sinful men, and they have abundantly left the traces of their mortality and sin. But in that Church, whether for judgment or for blessing, or rather, surely, for *both*—in it, in its core, in its unshaken depths, was the life and energy of the kingdom of God: never was the sense of its reality lost, never the faith in its King quenched; in the worst days of rebuke and blasphemy, from many an unknown altar, and many an unknown and humble heart, "hidden privily by *His* presence from the provoking of all men; kept secretly in *His* tabernacle from the strife of tongues," the songs of the kingdom of God went up unceasingly, witnessing to its continuous presence, telling of trust and love undisturbed, till the storm passed and the days were better. For the sake of the purposes and victories of the kingdom of God, the Church was set up by its Master, Christ; for the sake of them it continues to be; the reason of its existence is that we believe Christianity to be not a historical phenomenon, not a philosophy, not a mass of precepts and principles for individuals to choose from, but a divine religion. Forget that, and all is confusion in our thought of the Church. Remember that, and nothing of outward event or outward interference can take from her what she is.

But the Church cannot help on one side of it touching human society, its interests and its changes. That kingdom of God, for whose purposes the Church exists, cannot be moved. But the Church must have a human history. It may easily have to share the vicissitudes of those earthly things in which, at each moment of time, its lot may be cast. The course of its history at times has run parallel with that of human society, and in association with it—for human society, too, is part of the kingdom of God, and God takes care of what is His creation and watches over it in its best days and its worst. But so also the Church may find itself at cross purposes with the prevailing forces of society. We could hardly expect but that it must sometimes be so, when the invisible interests of the world to come find themselves in contact with the powers and interests of this world. Such moments may be, and have been, moments of great trial, well or ill borne, wisely or unwisely passed through. We cannot help seeing signs—they may be exaggerated, they cannot be said to be fanciful—that such a critical time may yet, sooner or later, be within our experience.

Before such times come, it is well to consider, calmly and devoutly, what should be the temper and attitude of the Church when apparently called to prepare for the possibility of grave changes, it may be, great disadvantages, in its outward condition.

The first thing to remember and to imprint on our minds is that these changes in condition are in themselves *outward* things; and that the Church, though we see its members, and worship in its shrines, and handle its property, and teach in its schools, and join in its administration, is in itself—in the "soul and being of its life,"[1] the spiritual body of its invisible Lord and Bridegroom, the "house not made with hands"—to be the "temple of the Holy Ghost;" a visible, a historic body indeed, but whose words are worse than idle unless it exists primarily and above all things for ends which are beyond this world, and is kept alive and shaped by influences which are not of this world. The Church, as we speak of it here, is first and above all things a religious society for religious ends; part, in time and in place, of that universal religious society which Jesus Christ created among men, and for whom and to whom He gives gifts for the blessing of the world. It seems a commonplace; but it is not so easy to translate it into a master principle of all judgment and all action in everything that relates to the Church. Yet it is only with a vivid and

[1] Wordsworth, *Excursion*, Book iv.

ever-present sense of what the Church really is, and what it exists for, that we can rise to the height of any fitting and adequate and worthy argument as to the importance of outward things and their action on her proper interests.

But outward things may affect her very deeply. Outward things may be the machinery created and committed to her by her Master, to be used, as the time requires, for the ends of the kingdom of God. She has no more right to make light of that machinery, or to surrender it, than she could have the right to say that she could not do her Master's work without it. She has it; it is confessedly very powerful for the ends she is bound to seek; she cannot, without cowardice, without ignominy, affect not to care about it, at the first summons of hostility, or ignorance, or indifference. Surely we may be pardoned if the prospect, even distant, of vast and unknown changes in the relations of the Church to society make us anxious. Surely it need not be personal position or material interests which must be supposed to fill all our thoughts at the chances of a possible great break-up, a tearing up of what has been so familiar to all of us—so precious and venerable to some of the noblest and best among us. A far-reaching unsettlement, which must cripple and embarrass religious work, which must humble the Church and the religion which the Church teaches, in the eyes of the world, may well stir the hearts of Churchmen who, if earthly loss could further the kingdom of God, or might even make human society go more smoothly and more righteously, would not shrink from saying that the Church had better resign itself to sacrifice what is its own of outward things. But such a result has not been made probable yet. And there can hardly be said to be such an exclusive sense of justice, such exclusive sympathy with high purposes, such manifest and equitable intelligence of all the bearings of the case, on the side of those who call for change, that Churchmen, who are Englishmen also, should not put their objections to it as strongly as they honestly and truthfully may, on the ground of civil right and social benefit; should not shrink from lightly venturing on so tremendous an experiment on the moral and spiritual forces to which we are accustomed in England; should not resist what seems to them a great wrong.

Who has a right to complain of such resistance? Yet, after all, what *we* have to remember is, that the object of our interest is not merely a great and time-hallowed institution, bound up with the history and character of English society, but the Church of Christ among us, the "Church of the living God." It is that which we have to think for; it is that for whose welfare we are in our day responsible; it is that for which, if there is danger, we must strive. It is high spiritual interests that we have to guard; the highest that we can conceive among us—the faith, the spirit, the gifts, the life of what we believe to be Christ's Holy Catholic Church. This high idea of what we mean by the Church is not only the true one, not only the one really worthy the enthusiasm of Churchmen, but it is the safest and most powerful appeal to the thoughts of reasonable men. It was this that in days of danger fifty years ago— the revival of the great idea of the Church, the extrication of it, in its religious and spiritual significance, from the earthly associations which had encumbered and obscured it—it was this which in spite of great difficulties, great troubles, great disasters, staved off the dangers, and infused new life and elevation and strength into all our religion.

After all, our Master has said, "My kingdom is not of this world." No words have been so misused, with such blind inconsistency and recklessness of their recoil, so that they seemed to hit an opponent. But there they are, all the same; they mean much for *us*, however they may be misquoted by others :—

"This is a text," says an impressive writer,[1] "which has, as it were, looked at the Church ever since the Church was founded. It is like an eye fixed upon her, from which she cannot escape. . . . Go where she will, and in whatever divergent paths, and branches of those paths, and circuits of those paths, that eye has been upon her. . . . That saying has looked through history, on all the successive phases of the Church's worldly position."

It has looked, and often in vain. But there the words stand, with their warning to us.

[1] Dr. Mozley, *University Sermons*, Sermon I.

They warn us as to the methods, as to the temper, as to the reasonings, with which we wage our warfare for the Church of Christ. They warn us that there may be many ways legitimate, or at any rate customary, in questions of this world, which do not become those who are contending for what is *not* of this world. They warn us not to lose our sense of the realities of the kingdom of God, even in our zeal for its honour; not to lose our sense of proportion, even in asserting its claim to what is its own, to what cannot without wrong be taken from it. They bid us keep watch over our hearts and lips; to be just to others, even if they are unjust to us; to leave to those who will the language of passion or exaggeration, much more of recrimination and insult; to remember to *whom* it was said, "Ye know not what spirit ye are of;" to remember *where* it is said, "The wrath of man worketh not the rightcousness of God." And, above all, they warn us against a temptation which has before now come in the path of the Church, and may again—the temptation of paying too high a price to gain or to retain the advantages of this world. There are few among us with knowledge so large and thought so comprehensive as to be able to take in the full measure of the blessing of a Church like ours, which can speak to the nation as nothing else can, which holds such a machinery for good in its hands. But we may be asked to pay too highly for keeping what we so value. We may be asked to give up in exchange what we have no right to part with; to barter things that concern the life of the Church as a religious body; to turn the Church which we have received into something different; to consent to precipitate experiments and ill-considered compromises; to rush, under the alarm and perhaps danger of the moment, into projects of hasty change, in the hope of stopping a cry. Let us do our best; let us try to leave things better than we found them in the Church and in the world; let us "quit us like men," men of sense, men of courage, if we are forced into a struggle which must be a trying and a stern one; but let us remember, amid all its fortunes, *Who* has said, "*My* kingdom is not of this world."

Only let us do nothing unworthy of that "kingdom of God" in which we serve, to which we trust, and which has in it all our hopes. We are like soldiers in a vast, widely extended battlefield, wrapped in obscurity; in a fluctuating conflict of which we know not the phases, of which we seem utterly powerless to control the issues; but we *are* responsible for our own part; whatever goes on elsewhere, let us not fail in that. The changes of the world, which men think that they are bringing about, are in the hands of God. With Him, when we have done our duty, let us leave them. Only may we have grace from the Merciful and the True, before Whom St. Paul bent his knee, to "know how we ought to behave ourselves in the house of God, which is the Church of the living God, the pillar and ground of the truth;" remembering what is that Truth of truths which the Church exists to keep and to preach—"Without controversy, great is the mystery of godliness: God was manifest in the flesh, justified in the Spirit, seen of angels, preached unto the Gentiles, believed on in the world, received up into glory."

IV.

HOPE.

"And now abideth faith, hope, charity, these three."—
1 CORINTHIANS xiii. 13.

"FAITH, hope, charity"; these, in St. Paul's analysis, are the characteristic elements of the Christian mind. In the technical language of the Church they are the three theological virtues in contradistinction to the purely moral ones. They have filled a large space in the philosophy and the poetry of ancient Christendom, as an exhaustive co-ordination of the distinctive qualities of Christian saintship. St. Paul, as we know, in enumerating them, makes one of them the greatest in order and in nature—"the greatest of these is charity." But it is a first and foremost place among equals. All stand together, as nothing else does, in the front rank of the perfections which make Christian goodness. All are equally indispensable in those who would please God and follow Christ.

The question occurs to us sometimes, more or less consciously, why hope should be ranked so high, placed on a level with faith and charity. We can understand why faith should be so singled out; it is the foundation of the whole structure of religion; it is the bond between the creature and his invisible Maker and God; it is the special title of his acceptance; it is the ground of his self-devotion and obedience, of his highest and noblest ventures. Still more can we understand it of charity; for charity brings us near, in the essential qualities of character, to Him Whom we believe in and worship;

charity is the faint and distant likeness of Him Who so loved the world that He gave His only-begotten Son to save it; charity must last and live and increase, under whatever conditions the regenerate nature exists, the same in substance, however differing in degree, in the humblest penitent on earth and in the adoring saint or seraph in the eternal world. But hope is thought of, at first sight, as a self-regarding quality; something which throws forward its desires into the future, and dwells on what it imagines of happiness for itself. And hope, of all things, is delusive and treacherous; it tempts to security and self-deceit; it tempts us to dreams which cannot be realised, which divert us from the necessary and wholesome realities which *do* concern us: it is the mother of half the mistakes, half the fruitless wanderings, half the unhappiness of the world. How comes it that such a quality is placed on a level with faith and love? What need of encouragement to what men are only too ready to do of themselves?

But it is not really strange that St. Paul should raise hope to a Christian temper of the first order. St. Paul was a student of Scripture and of the history of his people and of religion in the world. And what is on the surface of the Bible is the way in which from first to last it is one unbroken, persistent call to hope—to look from the past and present to the future. Its contents, we know, are manifold and various; the subjects which it treats are widely different, and it is different in different parts of it in its way of treating them; it is the record of enormous changes, of a great progressive advance in God's dispensations and of man's light and character, of the long and wonderful education of the Law and the Prophets; its story of uninterrupted tendency is strangely chequered in fact; bright and dark succeed one another with the most unexpected turns —lofty faith and the meanest disloyalty, great achievements and unexpected failure, lessons of the purest goodness and most heartfelt devotion, with the falls and sins of saints, blessing and chastisement, the patience of God, and the incorrigible provocations of His people. In spite of all that is wonderful and glorious in it, it sounds like the most disastrous and unpromising of stories; and yet that is not its result. For amid the worst and most miserable conditions there is one element which is never allowed to disappear—the strength of a tenacious and unconquerable hope. Hope, never destroyed, however overthrown, never obscured even amid the storm and dust of ruin, is the prominent characteristic of the Old Testament. All leads back to hope—hope of the loftiest and most assured kind, even after the most fatal defeats, of changes which seem beyond remedy. The last word is always hope. If ever it dies, it revives again, larger, more confident than before. It is implied in the very language and appeals of despair. Hope spreads its colours over the sacred Book, whose outlook and interest is always the future, which looks back to the past only as the ground and pledge of the great things to come. So has St. Paul described the purpose and effect of Scripture, for his words are as true of the New Testament as of the Old. It is to impress upon religion the temper, the obligation of hope. He may be said to have characterised Scripture as, above everything, the Book of Hope. "For whatsoever things were written aforetime were written for our learning; that we, through patience and comfort of the Scriptures, might have hope." Over all other voices in the Old Testament, voices of command, entreaty, warning, rebuke, threatening, of triumph and gladness, of sorrow and desolation, rises dominant the voice of consolation, the instant call to hope even against hope, which elevates and strengthens as well as reassures: "Comfort ye, comfort ye My people, saith your God. Speak ye comfortably to Jerusalem, and cry unto her, that her warfare is accomplished, that her iniquity is pardoned: for she hath received of the Lord's hand double for all her sins."

Hope, I say—the temper and virtue answering to and embracing great and worthy things hoped for—elevates and strengthens and inspires. This is why it is one of the great elements of the religious temper; this is why it ranks with faith and charity. It is one of the great and necessary springs of full religious action. There may be a faith almost without hope; a faith which believes on, though it can see nothing; a faith which refuses to be comforted, which will not let the distant picture of better things rise before it, but yet trusts, even in the darkness, to God's truth and goodness. It is the deep and awful faith of him who said, " Though He slay me, yet will I trust in Him "—of the cry, " My God, My God, why hast Thou forsaken Me?" It is the touching and childlike confidence of the prophet—" Although the fig-tree shall not blossom, neither shall fruit be in the vines; the labour of the olive shall fail, and the fields shall yield no meat; the flock shall be cut off from the fold, and there shall be no herd in the stalls: yet I will rejoice in the Lord, I will joy in the God of my salvation." But the human spirit can hardly stand long the strain of a hopeless faith; one or other of the elements will assert its supremacy. And hope is the energy and effort of faith; the strong self-awakening from the spells of discouragement and listlessness and despair. What gives its moral value to hope, what makes it a virtue and a duty, is that in its higher forms it is a real act and striving of the will and the moral nature; and if any one thinks that this is an easy process he has yet much to learn of the secrets of his own heart. It is an act, often a difficult act, of choice and will, like the highest forms of courage. It is a refusal to be borne down and cowed and depressed by evil; a refusal, because it is not *right*, to indulge in the melancholy pleasure, no unreal one, of looking on the dark side of things. It is so that hope plays so great a part in the spiritual life; that it fights with such power on the side of God. For it not only receives, not only welcomes, not only trusts in God's promises, but it throws into them light and reality; they become to it not words but substantial things. It is on our wild and wayward imagination that the forces play both of fear and hope; it is there that we conjure up dangers, that we allow ourselves to faint and be dismayed at the prospect and omens of coming trouble; it is there that we look forward and see all that we have loved and cared for come to nought. And on the other hand, hope, religious hope, is a deliberate counter-appeal to that mighty power which disposes with such mysterious influence of so much of human life. It is an endeavour to subject imagination to truth and reason and God. It is an exercise, it may well be, of self-mastery, to enlist imagination on the side of God, as the ally and enlightener and support of faith; to make it use its charms against dark dreams and terrors. And further, hope is a great instrument of spiritual and moral discipline. "We are saved by hope," says St. Paul. Long waiting, we know now, is God's appointed order for the generations of men. There was a time when men thought that all would soon be over; they mistook God's way. With all the ups and downs of earthly history the world holds on its course, and one after another men are born, and play their part, and die. All kinds of changes, all kinds of fortunes, befall His Church, befall us all who are going through our trial time. And we are often tempted to be tired and depressed, out of heart, and out of patience. Ah! my brethren, shall we answer to God's purpose, Who has bidden us hope, Who has given us ground for hope, so amazing, so blessed? Shall we let it make us what it was meant to make us—cheerful, calm, even-minded, large-hearted, generous? Shall we let its light and its brightness wean us from the dulness and heaviness of an unhopeful temper, rouse us to activity and the zest and gladness of charity, when we are fretted by little troubles, or oppressed by great ones? This is the office of hope; this is what it contributes to Christian excellence. It is not little. If only we hoped in earnest to be what St. Paul and St. John hoped to be; hoped in earnest, as they did, for the future of righteousness and glory which they held up to their disciples and to the generations of the Church, we should know more than we do, not only of their joy, but of their strength and their goodness.

This temper of hopefulness is not only concerned with the great things of hereafter. It has to do with our feelings towards things here. There must often be much in the course of things which interest us now, to distress and alarm us: evils which seem without remedy, defeats which seem final, perplexities through which we cannot see our way, dark and gloomy clouds rising in menace over our familiar world. To hope seems to us then like deluding ourselves; we call it optimism, an instinctive dislike to pain, a determination not to see the cruel truth. And yet how often has it appeared in the upshot of things that if in the darkest times any had been bold enough to hope he would have been amply justified? What must have been the feelings of Christians in the fourth and fifth centuries, when, just as Christianity seemed to have won its way into the Roman Empire, they saw the fierce northern barbarians break into it, and the heathen triumph over religion and civil order? Which would then have seemed the judgment of sober good sense—the despondency which only saw the frightful mischief, or the bold hope which saw in the barbarians the seed of a great Christendom? Yet, who would have been right and who wrong? Or again, in the tenth century, when open wickedness and ignorance filled the high places of the

Church, when all seemed so bad and so hopeless that men disposed of their goods as if the end of the world must come with the end of the century, if any one had looked forward, in spite of all, to Christians again recognising their high calling, again preaching peace and charity, and leaving all to follow Christ—to the return of a great intellectual tide of art and of thought, where now all was brutality and darkness—would he not have seemed a dreamer? Yet, who would have been wrong and who right—the dreamer or the despairing? And so of other times of confusion and corruption in the Church, when the powers of evil seemed impregnable, and the attempts of those who dared to cope with them seemed only to issue in disappointment, or new forms of mischief; amid the polished or superstitious godlessness of the fifteenth century, in the angry and heady disputations of the sixteenth, in the tumults and revolutions, the atrocious wars of religion in France and Germany, in the fierce cruelty, the depravity, the plundering greed of the upper classes, the depression and helplessness of the poor, left without guide or friend, the insolent claims, the savage intolerance of rival systems and rival teachers, were there not ample arguments for despair? and would he not have been a bold man, who could put his trust in the powers of self-correction and recovery, in the living gifts of the Holy Ghost, and hope that things would not always be as bad as this, that the days of peace and mercy would yet come? And who would, after all abatements, have been right? "It is come," wrote the soberest and also the loftiest of Christian thinkers in the last century, "I know not how, to be taken for granted by many persons, that Christianity is not so much as a subject of inquiry; but that it is now at length discovered to be fictitious." The ominous symptom has not certainly grown less ominous; but could even the calm and large mind of Bishop Butler have embraced the thought that with this, not diminished, perhaps aggravated, there might also come a steady growth of energy and fervour and deepening practical purposes in the Church and religious men, such as certainly he had not seen, nor could look for?

We are but short-sighted creatures. We see and feel so clearly what is immediate and pressing that we leave out of account all the subtle and complex forces, mighty and ever active, though we do not discern them, that are, perhaps, in the long run more eventful and decisive than anything we can now see. It is almost proverbial how often the prophecies of the wisest and most sagacious— prophecies of evil and of good, calm and deliberate forecasts which seem to rest on unanswerable reasons—are almost ludicrously falsified in the event. It is unsafe to prophesy; it is more than wise, it is our duty, to hope. God's mercy has never deserted us. It has allowed the darkest hours to pass over us, the severest trials, the keenest and bitterest sorrows. His returning mercy has come back, perhaps in a very different form from what we expected; it has not restored what was lost; it has not revived what had perished; but it has given us something to take the place of what is gone. He has varied the conditions of our service. But He has come back to us in mercy; come back to us in His bounty and quickening grace; come back to us in His manifold, His inexhaustible wisdom, bringing new good strangely out of surmised evil, compensating, refashioning, developing, adapting. Surely this is the wonderful experience of our most disappointing and disobedient and yet enduring Christendom. We need not blind ourselves to facts; we have our part to do, and must deal as we may and as we ought with what is dangerous and hurtful. But the God of Hope calls to us out of the darkness; and we are unfaithful to Him if in our distress and fear we shut our ears to His voice, and dwell despondingly on a future which is in His hands.

But to Christians all that here invites and demands hope is but little to that which is to be when all here shall have been passed and over. It is simply the most literal fact that God has set before us, in another state of being, the most wonderful future, which is within the certain reach of every single one of us: as much, as certainly within our reach, as anything that we know of, which we could obtain to-morrow. This is the plain, clear, certain promise, without which Christianity is a dream and delusion. The life and destiny of each individual man runs up to this; this is what he was made for; for this he has been taught, and has received God's grace, and has been tried, and has played his part in the years of time. It is the barest of commonplaces; and yet, I think, to any one who has tried to open his mind to its reality and certainty, it must have come with a strange and overpowering force—new on every fresh occasion, like nothing else in the world. For it is one thing to look forward to some great general event, the triumph of the saints of God, the final glory of the great company of the redeemed; one thing to look at all this from the outside, as a spectator by the power of imagination and thought: and quite another, when it comes on your mind that you yourself in the far-off ages, you yourself, the very person now on earth, are intended to have your place—your certain and definite place—in all that triumph, in all that blessedness, in all that glory; and yet surely, to any one that will, this is the prospect; this, and nothing less. You may put Christianity aside; you may say that such hopes cannot be for man; but, if you are a Christian, this in its utmost fulness and reality is what you are to hope for. Think of anything you most long for here; you see perhaps the day—weeks or months or years hence—when you shall have the great desire on which you live. So in all sober assurance and serious meaning the New Testament bids us look forward to that future which one day we are to reach. What will be those new conditions of our being, which are one day to be as familiar to man's perfected nature as the conditions of sin and suffering are familiar to him now, we cannot tell. "Eye hath not seen, nor ear heard, neither hath it entered into the heart of man, the things which God hath prepared for them that love Him." How could it be otherwise? How can we imagine that the experience of our short years in this life, strange and wonderful as it is, could be the measure of a state of being in which we are to be brought near to Jesus Christ, and are to share the life of immortality? It is shown in Scripture, in figure and emblem—figure and emblem which blind us with their glory, even while they transport us with rapture; yet only in figure and emblem could such things be presented to the mind of man. But some things are certain, which we can understand even now. Then, at last, we may dare to look forward to being sinless. Think of what you know of your own conscience, your own temptations, your own falls, your own struggles for forgiveness and restoration; and then think what it will be, to have left all that behind. Then, whatever be the functions and employment of that perfect state, whatever work God may have for us to do, we shall have the will and the power to do it as the angels do. The divided service, the broken purpose, the double mind, the treacheries of the will, the blindness of self-deceit, the laggard indolence, all that now mars and cripples our sincerest obedience, will then have been purged away, and in all the fulness of truth we shall know how to serve Him with a whole heart. Again, the greatest and purest and most enduring happiness we can know here is in the exercise of the affections; there, in infinite measure, will be all that calls forth human affections, and there human affections will be raised to new power and strength—transfigured, purified, glorified. And then, in ways we cannot dream of now, we shall be brought near to Him from Whom we have our being, God our Father, the Ever-Blessed and the All-Holy, and Jesus Christ Who loved and saved us, and that Holy Spirit which has been with us all the days of our wandering here. And those strange words shall be fulfilled which promise that "We shall be like Him; for we shall see Him as He is."

This, as no one denies, is what Scripture invites us to believe and to hope. These are no idle exaggerations of rhetoric or fancy; they are the bare words of truth and soberness. It is what we are living for, unless we are living in vain. And with such things before us, with such things showed to us, can we wonder that the Apostle places hope, the temper that embraces this and rejoices in this, on a level with faith and charity? Have such things been told us for nothing? Are they things to be without a meaning to us? Have we, as we have, the power, in some degree at least, of realising them, of projecting our very self, our character, our feelings, our conscious being into this amazing future, reserved and waiting for us; of imagining how we shall feel there; and can we have been meant to live as if those things were not? Is it not *simply a duty* to hope; a sin against God's high goodness, a crime against the order of His teaching, not to hope? Is it not a duty, in solemn and quiet self-recollection, to put before our thoughts that unbroken and continuous line, which joins this very present moment with that hour which certainly is to arrive, when we *must* be changed, when we *may* be changed into the spotless blessedness of the saints of God? You—you yourself—with your trouble, your temptations, your sin, small or great, your conscious weakness, your insensibility and ignorance; yet you yourself are one of those of whom, if you will, all this wondrous future will, must, come true. There is no blessedness of the soul of man, no rest from weariness, no refreshment after toil, no opening of the eyes to beauty never seen by mortal eye, no delight in goodness, no rejoicing in perfect love, no ineffable sense of the sweetness and tenderness of God's mercy—none of these that may not be hoped for; hoped for with all the warrant of the Almighty's promise, by each soul here present, with its identity unbroken, with that individual character which makes it what it is. And is that great hope to be practically all a blank to us?

It is not to be told how much we lose of strength, of gladness and enlargement of heart, of power to do God's service cheerfully and happily, by not realising and dwelling on the great hopes "set before us." We let ourselves be blinded, fretted, disheartened by the present, because we will not look up and see what is as certain as the present, in the not very distant future. Many of us, to-day, remember with more or less regret that this is the last Sunday of the year; that another year has gone out of our tale of days. *Its* days are gone and will never come back; nor that which they brought, and took away with them; the pleasant times which those days gave us, the glad meetings, the sunny holidays, are gone; gone, with the happiness which its days wrecked, with the health that they have broken, with the old friends, the lives, some of them noble and precious ones, which they have taken with them into the past. Here, as at a deathbed, we feel the close of all earthly things, the inevitableness and the drawing near of death. With us the natural thing is to look back to the past; the word that naturally rises to our lips is, "Another year gone." It is natural with us: with St. Paul it is just as natural to reflect, " Now is our salvation nearer than when we first believed. The night is far spent, the day is at hand." It *is* the last Sunday, and that must give us much to think of. But it is not only, it is not chiefly that. About us are the songs, and the joy, and the innocent gladness of Christmas. About us, as we are reminded to-day, are the "bright beams of light which God casts upon His Church"[1]—bright indeed to us now, but only the faint quivering of the dawn of that Eternal Day. We, at least, if we are not Christians in vain, can join the stern and awful thoughts that accompany the lapse of time—ample enough, indeed, to make the boldest anxious—with the deep and chastened sense of realities beyond it, certain, final, ineffable, over which time has no power, which are warranted to men. We can pass on to the great hope which from end to end fills the Bible—the hope which ennobles and gladdens our mortal life; such

[1] Collect for St. John the Evangelist's Day.

a hope as carried St. Paul in strength and joy through the long "daily dying" of his Apostleship, and burst forth in such impassioned yet most reasonable conviction—"For I count," he says, "that the sufferings of this present time are not worthy to be compared with the glory that shall be revealed in us. . . . For I am persuaded, that neither death, nor life, nor angels, nor principalities, nor powers, nor things present, nor things to come, nor height nor depth, nor any other creature, shall be able to separate us from the love of God, which is in Christ Jesus our Lord."

THE END.

Printed by R. & R. CLARK, *Edinburgh.*

www.ingramcontent.com/pod-product-compliance
Lightning Source LLC
Chambersburg PA
CBHW020123170426
43199CB00009B/617